Is it smooth or rough?

Heather Rising

Crabtree Publishing Company

www.crabtreebooks.com

Author: Heather Rising
Publishing plan research and development:
  Sean Charlebois, Reagan Miller
  Crabtree Publishing Company
Project development: Clarity Content Services
Project management: Karen Iversen
Project coordinator: Kathy Middleton
Editors: Heather Rising, Trudy Rising, Kathy Middleton
Copy editor: Dimitra Chronopoulos
Proofreader: Reagan Miller
Design: First Image
Photo research: Linda Tanaka
Prepress technician: Katherine Berti
Print and production coordinator: Katherine Berti

Photographs:
p1 JazzBoo/shutterstock; p4 Noel Hendrickson/Thinkstock; p5
monkeybusinessimages/BIGSTOCK; p6 left clockwise Andrey Eremin/
shutterstock, Arkady/shutterstock, Johan63/dreamstime.com; p7 top
Sonyae/BIGSTOCK, Nattika/shutterstock; p8 Hemera/Thinkstock;
p9 Hemera/Thinkstock; p10 Look!/BIGSTOCK; p11 istockphoto/
Thinkstock; p12 left Lasse Kristensen/shutterstock, Sadeugra/iStock;
p13 Hemera/Thinkstock, iStockphoto/Thinkstock; p14 left Simon
Valentine/BIGSTOCK, Mircea Bezergheanu/shutterstock; p15
iStockphoto/Thinkstock; p16 top Moth/dreamstime.com, Loretta
Hostettler/iStock; p17 Nekrasov Andrey/shutterstock; p18 left
Zimmytws/ BIGSTOCK, geoM/shutterstock; p19 iStockphoto/
Thinkstock; p20 left Kmiragaya/BIGSTOCK, lightkeeper/BIGSTOCK;
p21 left clockwise Eliza Snow/iStock, Andras Csontos/iStock,
Atti Tibor/shutterstock; p22 top left clockwise Hayward Gaude/
dreamstime.com; Atiketta Sangasaeng/shutterstock; Yargin/
shutterstock; 333DIGIT/shutterstock; Olivier Le Moal/shutterstock,
RTimages/shutterstock; cover shutterstock

Library and Archives Canada Cataloguing in Publication

Rising, Heather
  Is it smooth or rough? / Heather Rising.

(What's the matter?)
Includes index.
Issued also in electronic formats.
ISBN 978-0-7787-2051-5 (bound).--ISBN 978-0-7787-2058-4 (pbk.)

  1. Materials--Texture--Juvenile literature. 2. Friction--Juvenile
literature. 3. Matter--Properties--Juvenile literature. I. Title.
II. Series: What's the matter? (St. Catharines, Ont.)

TA418.5.R57 2012   j620.1'129   C2012-900297-6

Library of Congress Cataloging-in-Publication Data

Rising, Heather A.
Is it smooth or rough? / Heather Rising.
p. cm. -- (What's the matter?)
Includes index.
ISBN 978-0-7787-2051-5 (reinforced library binding : alk. paper) --
ISBN 978-0-7787-2058-4 (pbk. : alk. paper) -- ISBN 978-1-4271-7949-4
(electronic pdf) -- ISBN 978-1-4271-8064-3 (electronic html)
1. Matter--Properties--Juvenile literature. 2. Surfaces (Physics)--Juvenile
literature. 3. Surface roughness--Juvenile literature. I. Title.

QC173.16.R57 2012
620.1'1292--dc23
                              2012000122

Crabtree Publishing Company

www.crabtreebooks.com   1-800-387-7650

Printed in the U.S.A./032012/CJ20120215

Published in Canada
Crabtree Publishing
616 Welland Ave.
St. Catharines, ON
L2M 5V6

Published in the United States
Crabtree Publishing
PMB 59051
350 Fifth Avenue, 59th Floor
New York, New York 10118

Published in the United Kingdom
Crabtree Publishing
Maritime House
Basin Road North, Hove
BN41 1WR

Published in Australia
Crabtree Publishing
3 Charles Street
Coburg North
VIC 3058

What is in this book?

What is matter?

Everything you see is made of **matter**.

Clouds, birds, and trees are matter.
Even bubble gum is matter.

Matter takes up space and has **mass**.

Mass is the amount of material in an object.

Matter has different **properties**.

Properties describe how something looks, feels, tastes, smells, or sounds.

What properties do these flowers have?

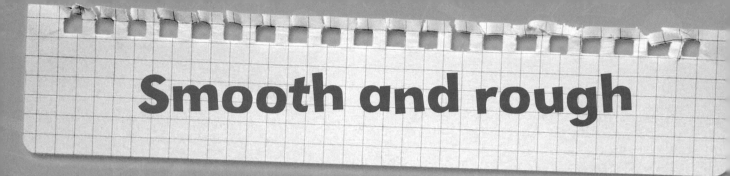

One property of matter
is how it feels.

Some matter feels smooth.

Some matter feels rough.

bump   groove

Rough matter has
a lot of bumps
and grooves.

6

Smooth matter has no bumps.

We can also use the word **texture** to describe how something feels when we touch it.

What texture does this squash have?

The top of a table is smooth.

You can slide your hand across it.

There are no bumps or grooves to stop your hand from moving across it.

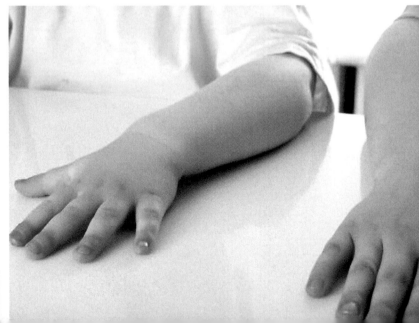

Look carefully at the apple.

Does the apple have bumps?
What is its texture?

What is rough?

A pineapple is covered in many bumps and grooves.

When you move your hand over the skin, you can feel its rough texture.

10

Which of these foods
are smooth and
which ones are rough?

Which textures help?

The tops of tables are smooth.

So are dishes. There are no places for dirt to hide.

Smooth things are easy to clean.

The pot scrubber feels rough. When it rubs against a pot, its bumps scrape the pot clean.

Bedtime things

Feel your toothbrush bristles. The rough bristles scrub your teeth clean.

bristles

Your pillowcase is smooth. There are no bumps to scratch your cheek. You can have a good night's sleep.

Look around your room. What do you have that is smooth? What do you have that is rough?

Friction

Friction is how hard or easy it is to rub two objects together.

Objects with smooth surfaces, such as ice, make less friction than objects with rough surfaces.

Smooth objects can move quickly.

When rough things rub together, the bumps and grooves catch on each other. This slows them down.

This truck has rough tires. It will not roll fast over bumpy stones.

You will have to push it hard to move it over the stones.

Friction outside

Look at the bottom of your running shoes. The bumps and grooves are called the tread.

The tread rubs against the ground and makes friction. Friction slows you down so you will not slip.

tread

The slide has no bumps. There is less friction between you and the slide. You can slide down fast.

Inside and outside

It is easy to slide on ice because it is smooth. Ice can be dangerous.

Sometimes sand is put on top of an icy road.

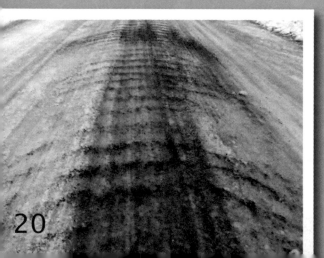

Sand is rough and increases friction. Cars and people will not slip.

Rollerblade wheels roll quickly. Are the wheels smooth or rough?

Bicycle tires are rough. When you ride on a slippery path, friction stops your tires from sliding.

What other smooth things go fast? What other rough things help slow us down?

21

What do you think?

These objects are smooth.

Why are they smooth?

These objects have a rough texture.

Why are they rough?

WELCOME

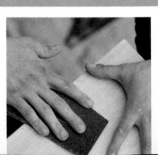

Words to know and Index

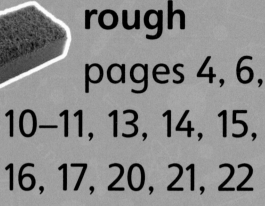

Notes for adults

Objectives

- to introduce children to the concept of matter
- to help children learn to compare and contrast
- to help children differentiate between smooth and rough
- to help children think about the use of different textures

Prerequisite

Ask children to read *Is it heavy or light?* and *Is it hot or cold?*
These titles introduce the concept of matter. They also reinforce the idea of comparing and contrasting objects.

Questions before reading *Is it smooth or rough?*

"Can you name something that is smooth?"

"Can you name something that is rough?"

"Can you guess how something feels just by looking at it?"

Discussion

Read the book to the children or share the reading with them. Discuss the food we eat. "How does it feel in your mouth?" Use crackers and pudding as examples to get you started. Make a chart and list different foods as smooth or rough. "When you have a sore throat, do you like to eat certain foods?"

Discuss the clues our eyes give us about something's texture.

Extension

Discuss friction. Have the children try rubbing their hands together. Our hands have small bumps on them that slow them down when we rub them together.

Can the children rub their hands together hard enough to make heat?

Let the children try using sandpaper on wood. Let them feel the wood after they have sanded it. This will demonstrate how friction can generate heat. This will also demonstrate how something rough can be used to make something smooth.